YOUR BOOK OF ACTING

The YOUR BOOK Series

Acting
Aeromodelling
Animal Drawing
Aquaria
Astronomy
Badminton
Bridges
Butterflies and Moths
Cake Making and Decorating
Camping
The Way a Car Works
Card Games
Card Tricks
Chemistry
Chess
Computers
Confirmation
Contract Bridge
Mediaeval and Tudor Costume
Seventeenth and Eighteenth Century Costume
Nineteenth Century Costume
Dinghy Sailing
The Earth
Electronics
Embroidery
Engines and Turbines
The English Bible
Fencing
Figure Drawing
Fishes
Flower Arranging
Flower Making
Flying
Freshwater Life
Furniture
Golf
Gymnastics
Hovercraft
The Human Body
Judo
Kites
Knitted Toys
Knitting and Crochet
Knots
Landscape Drawing
Light
Magic
Maps and Map Reading
Mental Magic
Modelling
Money
Music
Model Car Racing
Paper Folding
Parliament
Party Games
Patience
Pet Keeping
Photographing Wild Life
Photography
Keeping Ponies
Prehistoric Britain
Puppetry
The Recorder
Roman Britain
Rugger
The Seashore
Self-Defence
Sewing
Shell Collecting
Skating
Soccer
Sound
Space Travel
Squash
Stamps
Surnames
Survival Swimming and Life Saving
Swimming
Swimming Games and Activities
Table Tennis
Tape Recording
Television
Tennis
Trampolining
Trees
Underwater Swimming
Veteran and Edwardian Cars
Vintage Cars
Watching Wild Life
Waterways
The Weather
Woodwork

YOUR BOOK OF
ACTING

KENNETH NUTTALL

with illustrations by
JANET NUTTALL

FABER AND FABER LTD
3 Queen Square
London

*First published in 1958
by Faber and Faber Limited
3 Queen Square London WC1
Second impression 1961
Third impression 1966
Second edition 1972
Reprinted 1973
Printed in Great Britain by
Latimer Trend & Co Ltd Plymouth
All rights reserved*

ISBN 0 571 04668 1

© *1958 by Kenneth Nuttall*

CONTENTS

Introduction	*page* 9
Moving	11
Lazy Ali — A Mime	20
Speaking	25
Some Do's and Don'ts for Actors	30
How To Produce A Play	34
Costumes	44
Make-Up	49
Lighting	55
Making Your Own Play	63
Improvised Drama	74

PLATES

1. Boys acting a classical theme   *facing page* 32
2. Children acting the story of *Orpheus and Eurydice*   32
3. The 'slashing downwards' movement applied to a dramatic situation   33
4. The 'pressing upwards' movement   33
5. Boys acting a Mime about black magic and Zombies in the jungles of Martinique   48
6. The Mad Hatter's Tea Party   48
7. 'The Producer should plan the positions of the players . . . so that they form a series of interesting groupings'   49
8. A Youth Club's production of *Treasure Island*   49

ACKNOWLEDGEMENT

The author gratefully acknowledges his indebtedness to Mr. Alan Garrard of the Woodberry Down Secondary School for permission to use the photographs illustrated in Plates 1, 2, 5 and 7.

Plates 3 and 4 are from photographs taken by T. H. Greville of Watford.

INTRODUCTION

There is no need to tell you of the pleasure that can be derived from acting. You know all about that, for you have all been acting since you were very small. You probably started by 'being' somebody—you were Mother, or Father, or an engine-driver, or a bus-conductor. Later, with your friends, you were Robin Hood in Sherwood Forest, cowboys in the wild west, Red Indians on the prairie, pirates on the high seas and soldiers in battle. You acted stories made up by yourselves and, no doubt, thought what great fun you were having! And so you were! Not only were you enjoying yourselves—you were learning at the same time.

These games formed a normal part of the process of 'growing up' and were played purely for your own pleasure. This little book is meant to help you so to improve your acting that your efforts may give pleasure to others as well as yourselves. Here you will find exercises to help you to move easily and freely; exercises to help you to speak expressively; and some suggestions on how to make your own plays. Also there are hints on producing a play, on make-up, lighting and costume.

In all dramatic activity it is important to remember that the movement and speech should come from within—they should be the outcome of feeling or emotion. When you are acting the part of a cruel old miser, you should try to *feel* cruel

Introduction

and *feel* old. If you are portraying a nurse tending a sick patient, you should feel gentle and tender. You should forget that you are you and feel that, for the time being, you really are the character you are pretending to be. If you can do this, your acting will be expressive and convincing.

It is hoped that the activities described in this book will not only give you pleasure and profit, but that they will inspire you to experiment and to make and produce plays of your own. But whether your activities are composed by yourselves or taken from some other source, remember that if a thing is worth doing, it is worth doing well, and the best results can be obtained only through perseverance and hard work. There is no short cut!

MOVING

Acting consists of three things:

          MOVING

          SPEAKING

          FEELING

—and first you must learn to move freely.

It is quite possible to tell a story by movement alone. By means of the expression on your face, the way you use your hands, the movement of your limbs and bodies, the audience can follow what you are trying to convey. The eyes and the hands are particularly expressive. For instance, wide-open eyes can express fear or horror or amazement, whilst hands can express aggressiveness (a clenched fist) or greed (fingers curled in a claw-like position) as well as many other characteristics and emotions. This art of telling a story by movement alone is called MIMING, and at the end of the chapter you will find a story which you and your friends can turn into a mime.

It is a mistake, however, to think too much about your movements and gestures when you are acting. The important thing is to *feel* the emotion behind the movement. If you *feel*

Moving

Aggressiveness   or   Greed

angry, you will automatically *move* angrily: if you *feel* afraid, you will *move* fearfully.

Each of us has his own sphere of movement. This is the airspace around us in which we are able to move our bodies and limbs. It is surprisingly large!

Stand with your feet comfortably apart. Imagine you are inside a large, glass bowl. If you stretch out your right arm to the side and, at the same time, bend your right knee, you can just touch the 'bowl' with your finger-tips. Similarly, by stretching the left arm and bending the left knee, you can touch the 'bowl' on that side. You can also touch the bottom of the 'bowl' (the floor), or the top of the 'bowl' by reaching up high, and, by placing one foot backwards and turning slightly, you can touch that part of the 'bowl' which is behind you.

Imagine the inside of your 'bowl' is dusty. Take two imaginary dusters—one in each hand—and polish the whole of the inside surface of the bowl.

Now move round the room, taking your bowl with you. As you move, touch the inner surface all over—high, low, at the sides, behind you.

Here are a few basic movement exercises. You can practise them alone or with your friends. All you need is space. Of

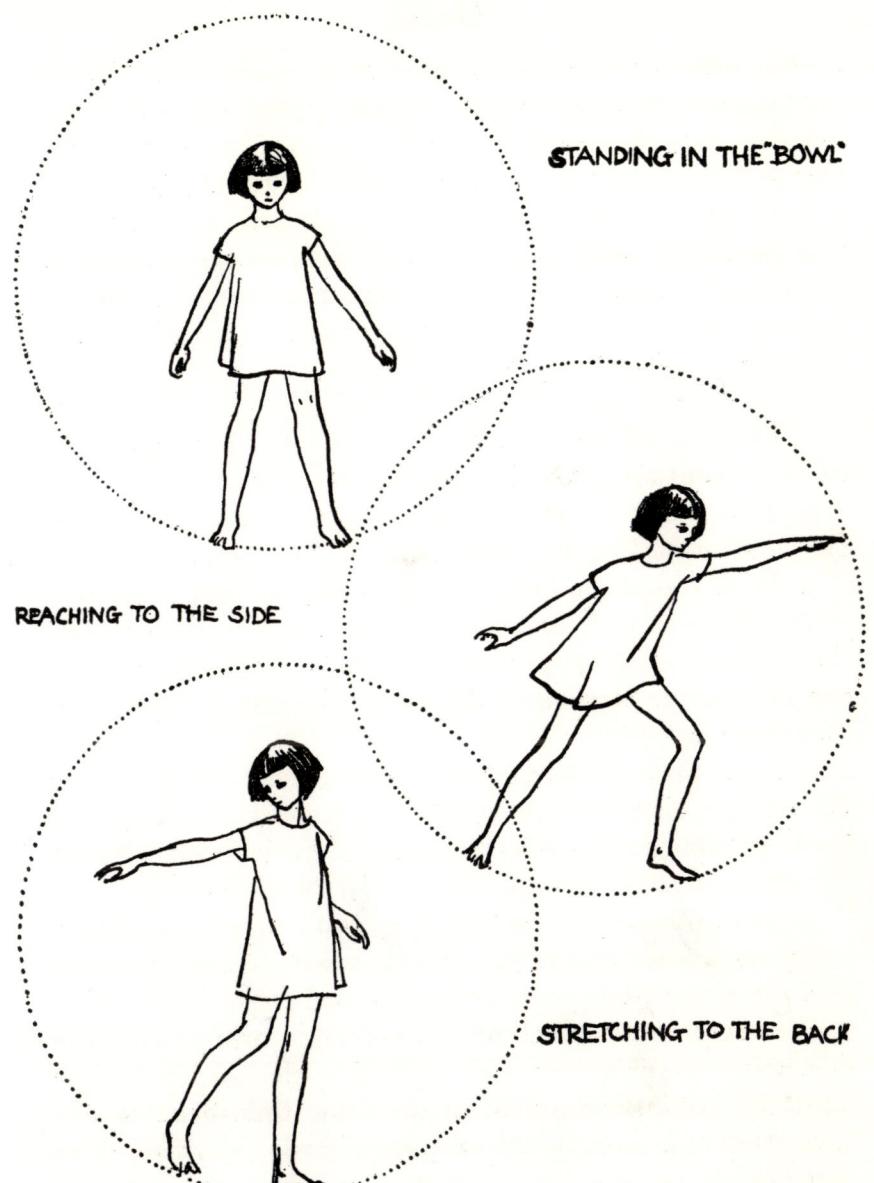

The Sphere of Movement

Moving

course, a large room with a good floor is best, but if this is not available they can be done almost as well out-of-doors on any smooth surface such as tarmac or on a lawn. You will enjoy the movements more and derive greater benefit from them if you remove as much of your outer clothing as possible so that your body and limbs may move with complete ease and freedom. Whatever movement you are practising, always bear in mind your 'sphere of movement'—that glass bowl which is so comfortably roomy!

1. Walk round the room. Feel the air with your finger-tips: feel it on your arms: feel it on your face.

2. Trot round the room filling as much space as you can. Use your arms, fingers, knees, head.

3. Walk round the room. As you walk, lift your arms sideways, upwards, over and, with flat palms, *press* downwards, (hands close together) at the same time leaning forward with one knee bent. Step one, two, three and *press!* Again, one, two, three and *press!*

4. Now, press upwards, just as if you were lifting a heavy box on to a high shelf. At every third step, go down, get the 'heels' of your hands under the box and lift it slowly—higher—higher—on to your toes—watch it! Feel its weight!

5. Now, similarly, press forwards, as if you were pushing a heavy motor-car which has broken down. Again, step one, two, three and *press!* One, two, three and *press!*

6. Next practise punching. As you step, bring your arms sideways, upwards, over and (with fists clenched and close together) *punch* downwards, at the same time bending one knee. Step one, two, three and punch hard! One, two, three and *punch!*

Moving

7. Now try punching upwards as though you were a goalkeeper punching high shots away with two fists.

8. Now try punching forward in the same way.

9. The next movement is a *slashing* movement. Step one, two, three and, as you step, bring the right hand up to near the left ear and, with fingers together and palm downwards,

make a slashing movement down, across and out to the right, as though you were cutting long grass with the outside edge of your hand. Let the other hand do what it seems to want to do. Now try with the left hand.

10. Next, try slashing in an upward direction. Start with the right hand across the body and near to the left hip. Bring hand across, up and out.

Moving

11. Folding inwards and stretching outwards. Stand still. Place the right foot back. Slowly sink down on to the right knee until you are sitting on your heel. At the same time, bring the arms round and fold them round your left knee. Drop your head. Feel that everything is going *inwards*. Now, slowly unfold and open out wide. On to your feet—arms open out, up and wide—feet apart and on to your toes—head up and then back! Stretch! Feel that everything is going *outwards*.

12. Lastly, move freely round the room using any combination of the movements you have practised. You might alternate punching upwards with punching downwards, or pressing upwards with slashing downwards, or you might combine three or four different movements.

Moving

The next step is to add imagination to your movements. Here you are beginning to *act*.

1. You are a carpenter. Take an imaginary saw and cut through a large piece of wood. (Use a stool or chair to represent the sawing-bench and on which to rest your knee.) *Feel* the smooth, wooden handle of the saw in your hand and the resistance as it cuts through the timber.

2. You are a postman, delivering letters in a street. Open the garden gate of each house, put the mail through the letter-box and rat-tat on the door. Don't forget to close the gate as you come out!

3. You are a duchess serving tea in her drawing-room. Sitting at a small table, you pour the tea from a silver teapot and hand the cups, one at a time, to the footman who takes them to your guests.

4. You are an artist painting a landscape in the open air. You stand before your easel with the palette in your left hand and the brush in your right. You keep looking carefully at the scene before you as you paint it on the canvas.

5. You are an old, crippled beggar. You limp along the gutter with a little tin mug in your hand, begging for coppers from the passers-by.

6. You are a wizard (or a witch) concocting a magic brew. You squat by the bubbling pot over the fire and keep adding the ingredients—toad's legs, crushed spiders, larks' tongues and so on —stirring the mixture all the

Moving

while. Your eyes glow as you think of how you intend to use it when it is ready!

7. You are a detective, following a suspected criminal through a wood. You move stealthily from tree to tree, taking what cover you can, and keeping a watchful eye on your quarry, ahead.

8. You are a scarecrow who has, magically, been given the power to move. You walk about, woodenly and stiffly, remembering that you are made of sticks, straw and rags.

9. You are walking home from the office when it starts to rain. You put on your mackintosh and put up your umbrella. The rain comes faster and faster. Now it is a downpour! You step quickly but carefully over the puddles and mud until, at last, you arrive home. You shake the water off your umbrella, hat and coat and hang them up to dry.

10. You are walking along a field-path when, before you on the ground, you see a strange, metal object. You stop, bend down and look at it. Gingerly, you pick it up and examine it. Whatever can it be? Suddenly, you notice that it is ticking like a clock! Is it a bomb about to explode? In a panic, you throw it away as far as you can and run for your life!

11. You are a guest in an hotel. As you pass through the hall, you glance at the letter-rack to see if there are any letters

Moving

for you. Yes, there is one. You take it, open it and read it. The news it contains is very bad. Slowly you sink down on to a nearby couch. You are very thoughtful and worried.

12. The following exercise can be done by a group of you and your friends. You are all staring intently at a spot on the ground in the centre of the group. There is a tiny plant: it has just broken through the earth. Watch it! It is a magic plant. It grows very quickly. Watch it grow—up—up! Now it is as high as your face. Now it is taller. Now a beautiful pink flower bursts from the top. Watch it! How lovely it is! Now, gradually, the whole plant turns into a dreadful, ugly, evil thing! It writhes like a lot of snakes! You are afraid of it! You drop back (perhaps on to the floor) and hide your eyes from the awful sight!

LAZY ALI

A MIME

(Here is a story which you and your friends can mime. One of you must be the Narrator who tells the story, and, as he tells it, the others act it in movement, gesture and facial expression. The Narrator might be dressed in a long robe and wear large spectacles. He might read the story, apparently from a huge volume held before him.)

CHARACTERS

Fatima, a washerwoman
Ali, her son
Three beggars
People of the city
A baker

The SCENE is laid in Baghdad, many years ago.

(The Narrator enters and stands in the centre of the stage.)

NARRATOR: Listen to the tale of Ali, the lazy, good-for-nothing son of Fatima. And, as you listen, watch, too, for you shall see the tale unfold before your eyes—just as it happened many years ago in the ancient city of Baghdad.

(Music begins as the NARRATOR *moves to the side of the stage.)*

Here we see Fatima, the washerwoman, busy at her wash-

Lazy Ali

tub. See how she rubs the clothes to make them spotless and white for her customers. And there, lolling on the floor by the wall, is Ali, her son. What a lazy fellow he is! There he lies, idly whittling a stick with his knife, whilst his poor old mother works her fingers to the bone to keep him in food and clothing! Fatima is a patient soul, but sometimes her son's idleness is too much for her and her patience wears thin! See —she is looking at him now with sorrow—and exasperation too! She is determined to cure his laziness if she can. She wipes her hands on her apron and gets a silver coin from the jar on the bench. She approaches Ali. She urges him to get up. Slowly and reluctantly, he rises. She gives him the coin and tells him to make himself useful by running to the baker's shop across the Market Place and bringing back a loaf of bread. Look! Ali does not want to go, the idle rascal! His mother is angry! See how she threatens him!

Now we see Ali slip the coin into his pocket. He goes out into the street and along the Market Place. Who are these lame creatures squatting here? Why, they are beggars, asking for alms. See how they shake their filthy rags and exhibit their sores and deformities! Ali stands and watches them. One of the passers-by drops a coin on the ground. See how the beggars scramble for it!

Ali laughs and continues on his way, idly kicking the stones as he goes. But what is that rolling on the ground? It is the silver coin! There is a hole in his pocket and it has dropped through! He does not know! The hole has been there for days but he is too idle even to ask his mother to mend it!

Now he has reached the baker's shop. There is the baker among his loaves and cakes. Ali asks him for a loaf. The baker hands one to him and demands the money. Ali feels in

Lazy Ali

his pocket. Alas! The coin is gone! Where can it be? Ali protests that he is sure he had the money. The baker is suspicious! He takes back the loaf and orders Ali out of the shop. Ali retraces his steps, searching—searching for the lost silver coin. He cannot find it. The people buffet him and push him! See—the lad is so dejected—he sinks to the ground in despair! His eyes wander miserably round the Market Place until they rest on the three beggars still begging for alms on the pavement. Ali looks thoughtful. Now his eyes light up! He thinks, 'Ah! That is the way to get my money back, and much more as well! I will pretend to be a beggar! The passers-by will give me *dozens* of silver coins!'

What is the silly lad doing now? Why, he is tearing his good clothes to make them ragged! He is daubing his face with mud! He is ruffling his hair! He watches the beggars carefully. Now he is imitating them. The passers-by feel sorry for him. See how sadly they shake their heads at the thought of so young a boy forced to beg for his living! See—they shower coins upon him! How eagerly he picks them up!

Now Ali is rich! He has a whole handful of silver coins. Joyfully, he jumps up and—silly boy—puts the coins in his pocket. He has forgotten again about the hole! Watch how he skips and leaps about in his happiness! And see how the coins, one by one, roll out, unnoticed, into the mud!

Here he is at home again. He bursts in, eager to tell his mother the good news! Fatima looks up from her wash-tub. She is shocked! Can this filthy scarecrow be her son? Yes, it is! 'Where is the loaf?' she demands. Ali, smiling to think how pleased his mother shortly will be, says, 'I have no loaf!' 'Then,' says his mother, 'give me back my silver coin!'

Ali puts his hand into his pocket—Oh, woe! Woe! Woe!

Lazy Ali

Look—just look at his face! He pulls out the lining of his pocket and shows—nothing but the hole!

Now, Fatima falls into a rage! See—she takes the stick which Ali was whittling, and beats him and beats him round and round the house! Surely a just reward for his idle ways!

CURTAIN

SPEAKING

So far, we have considered and practised MOVEMENT. Now, let us consider SPEECH.

When speaking a part in a play there is one essential thing to bear in mind—your speech must be easily heard by the audience. If you mumble, 'talk through your teeth' or are in any other way slovenly in your speech, the members of the audience will either fail to hear you, or will hear you only by straining their ears. If they cannot hear you, or can hear only with difficulty, they will not be able to follow the story of the play and will become bored and restless.

Your speech, therefore, must be clear and easily heard. It is not necessary, however, to shout (unless, of course, the character you are portraying happens to be a loud-mouthed sort of person, or one who becomes extremely angry or frightened). If you sound the consonants clearly—especially the end letters of the words—and breathe at the proper places (not in the middle of a word or in the middle of a phrase) it is possible to speak quite quietly and yet be heard in the furthest corners of a large room. Some professional actors are so clever in this way that they can make a whisper heard in all parts of a large theatre. Be careful, however, not to overdo this sounding of consonants and mouthing of vowels. Exaggerated or over-emphasized speech merely

Speaking

sounds artificial and stilted. Your speech should be natural but not slovenly.

Another thing you should learn is to vary your speech. Sometimes you will have to speak quickly, sometimes slowly, sometimes loudly, sometimes softly. One part may demand a high-pitched voice, another a low-pitched voice. You may be required to speak boldly or timidly or sadly or joyfully or angrily or fearfully. It all depends on what kind of character you are portraying and how 'he' or 'she' is *feeling* at any particular moment. Your speech will vary according to the mood of the character, the meaning of what he is saying and the kind of person he is. For instance, if you are a boy playing the part of an old man telling some very exciting news to someone, your speech will be rather high-pitched and quick and the excitement of the occasion will be noticeable in your voice. If you are a girl playing the part, say, of a nun comforting a sick and worried person, you will speak softly, slowly and gently, the tenderness you feel sounding in your voice.

As in movement, the *feeling* behind the words is the important thing. If you *feel* sad, you will speak sadly: if you *feel* spiteful, you will sound spiteful.

The last, and most difficult, thing to learn is to *project* your voice over to the audience. This applies particularly when you are acting on a 'picture-frame' or proscenium stage, and means 'throwing' your voice, as it were, over to everyone in the audience. You sometimes find, when two people are acting together, that although they are both speaking softly, you hear one much more easily than the other. They both may be speaking equally clearly and yet you feel a compulsion to listen to one rather than to the other, and what he is saying seems more interesting and more important. This is because

Speaking

one is *projecting* and the other is not. Again, it is largely a matter of *feeling*. The sincere actor who *feels* the emotions and who *feels* he really is the character he is portraying is much more likely to project than one who just speaks the words. So, although you may be speaking to another player who may be only six inches away from you, always keep in the back of your mind the fact that you are speaking not only to your fellow-actor, but also to the people in the back row of the audience who have bought their tickets and want their money's worth!

Here are a few speech exercises for you to practise:

1. Imagine you are Mrs. Smith, a housewife. Whilst dusting the parlour mantelpiece she is startled by a ball thumping against the window. This is the fourth time this has happened in the last half-hour. She feels very angry. Dropping her duster, she stamps to the front door and calls out:

'Now, look here, you boys! I've told you three times this morning and I'm not going to tell you again! Either take that blessed ball away and play somewhere else, or I'll set the police on you!'

Say the above as Mrs. Smith would have said it.

2. Imagine you are a prisoner who is being threatened by two brutal guards. One of the guards raises a gun and declares that he will shoot unless the prisoner tells them the names of his confederates. The prisoner, who, by this time, is exhausted, weak and very frightened, calls out:

'Don't shoot! I've had enough! I'll tell . . . I'll tell you everything, but don't shoot! *Please* don't shoot!'

3. Now imagine you are a Duchess whose son has just informed her that he wishes to become a clown in a circus. She says:

'But this is too ridiculous! Are you mad? A member of our

Speaking

family prancing and tumbling about in a circus-ring—the whole idea is absolutely preposterous!'

4. Now imagine you are a poor, unfortunate 'down-and-out' selling matches at a street corner. He whines:

'Box o' matches, mister? Buy a box, mister! Only twopence! 'Elp a poor starvin' bloke to earn an honest livin', sir!'

5. Now you are a lady who is staying as a guest in an old, rambling country house. She has just entered the living-room. Looking white and strained, she tells her host and his family that she has just seen what she believes to be a ghost on the landing. They disbelieve her. Becoming rather unnerved, she says:

'But I *did*, I tell you, I *did!* It was there as plain as anything! It had long, white fingers and its face . . . its face was . . . oh! it's too horrible!'

6. Now act the part of a headmaster (or headmistress) addressing the assembled school. He (or she) says:

'Before you go to your classes, there is a disturbing matter to which I must refer. I am extremely sorry to have to tell you that, somewhere in the school, we have a thief! Between three-thirty and four o'clock yesterday afternoon a valuable

Speaking

book was taken from Mr. Howarth's desk. Now, the sad thing about this business is that suspicion is thrown on everyone in the school!'

7. You are a 'Grandma'. Your little grandson has just been frightened by a big dog which barked and snapped at him. In a soothing, comforting voice, you say:

'There, there, there! Don't cry, love! The silly old dog's gone. He only wanted to play with you. That's all—just wanted to play with you a bit! Come on, now, let me dry your eyes. That's better. There's my brave boy!'

8. Finally, imagine you are a Christian slave in Ancient Rome. The cruel tyrants are about to throw you to the lions. A Roman officer has entered the cell in which you and your friends are imprisoned. You say to him:

'My friend, our hearts are full of sorrow—not for ourselves, but for you—and for Rome! We are not afraid! Neither you nor the Senate nor Nero himself can daunt us, for we are safe and secure in the arms of our God! Nothing you can do can touch us! You may mock, you may taunt, you may throw our poor, broken bodies to the lions, but we shall remain unbeaten and unafraid, for we are strong in the love of our Lord!'

SOME DO'S AND DON'TS FOR ACTORS

1. When you are on the stage you are 'in character'—that is, acting—all the time, whether you are speaking or not. When you are listening to another character speaking, let your face show what effect his words are having on you. This is called 're-acting'. However, be careful not to overdo the re-acting, or you may attract the audience's attention away from where it should be. Don't forget you are a member of a team, all working together.

2. When you are 'on-stage' but taking no part in the action of the play, STAND STILL or, if you are sitting, SIT STILL.

3. Don't fidget! If you don't know what to do with your hands, just let them hang loosely by your sides.

4. Avoid stiff little gestures and movements. When you have to make a gesture, let it be big and definite and be sure that it means something. (Remember how much room you have in your 'sphere of movement'.)

5. The gesture comes before the speech. Try this little exercise:

Say, 'That is the man!'—then point an accusing finger at an imaginary culprit.

Some Do's and Don'ts for Actors

Now, see how much more effective it is when you point the accusing finger *first*—then say, 'That is the man!'

6. Everything which happens on the stage should be *slightly larger than life*. Generally speaking, speech should be clearer and rather louder than ordinary conversation, movement and gesture should be bigger than the movement and gesture of everyday life, and facial contours and expression have to be emphasized by 'make-up'.

7. Everything done on the stage should have a purpose. Your speech, movement and facial expression should all help—

      (i) to build up and portray the character
or, (ii) to heighten the dramatic atmosphere
or, (iii) to carry the story along.

Suppose, for instance, you are playing the part of a rather fussy lawyer. If you occasionally take off your glasses and polish them with your silk handkerchief, you are using a gesture which is helping to build up and portray the character. It helps to show the audience that you are rather a fussy, meticulous kind of person. If you are playing a scene in a haunted house and you place your hand on your cheek and open your eyes wide, you are using a gesture which is helping to build up the dramatic atmosphere. If you go to a cupboard, open it, then run to the door and call to someone to come quickly to see what you have found, your movements are all helping to tell the story, or carry the plot along. If, however, you just wander about the stage for no reason, you are merely detracting the audience's attention from the real action of the play, and probably annoying the other actors at the same time!

8. Unless you are deliberately playing a slow scene, be *quick on your cues*. That means, begin to speak your lines as soon as the other actor has finished his. Don't allow pauses to occur

Some Do's and Don'ts for Actors

before you begin to speak unless the action of the play demands a pause. If you neglect this, you slow down the tempo of the acting and the audience may become bored.

9. When using a one-armed gesture, use the arm *away from the audience*. The pictures show how much better one looks than the other. Similarly, if you have to stand with one foot, say, on a step, let it be the foot *away from the audience.*

10. If you are facing sideways and have to turn to face the opposite direction, turn so that you face the audience on the way round.

11. It is NOT wrong occasionally to turn your back on the audience. Sometimes it can be very effective, and sometimes it is necessary. Remember, however, that if you speak with your back to the audience, your voice must be rather louder and your enunciation even clearer than when you are facing down-stage. Some actors are extremely clever at acting with their backs. The back of an actor's head can be

1. Boys acting a classical theme. Note the basic movements of pressing and thrusting

2. Children acting the story of *Orpheus and Eurydice*

3. The 'slashing downwards' movement applied to a dramatic situation

4. The 'pressing upwards' movement as it might be used in a pleading and supplicating situation

Some Do's and Don'ts for Actors

made to express a great deal, as can the way the body is held when viewed from behind.

12. Try to get light and shade into your acting by varying the pitch, tone, loudness and speed of the speech and the tempo of the movement. A play is rather like a picture. It needs colour, shadows and high-lights to make it vivid and interesting.

13. When playing comedy, remember to *wait for the laughs*. Don't try to go on speaking whilst the audience is still laughing loudly, or you will not be heard. The time to start speaking again is *just before the laugh has died out*. If you leave it too late, the action of the play will flag. This is called 'timing' and is very important. Timing, or beginning to speak at exactly the right moment when the audience is receptive and ready, cannot be taught. It is a matter of experience and instinct. Incidentally, it is possible to 'kill' an unwanted laugh which comes in the wrong place by making a sudden gesture or movement and speaking the next line firmly and rather quickly. This should be done as soon as the laugh starts.

14. Begin to use your 'hand-props' as early as possible during rehearsals so that you become familiar with the feel of them and able to handle them easily and confidently.

15. Never mingle with the audience during the intervals whilst you are still in costume and made-up. This is 'not done' and is considered bad manners.

HOW TO PRODUCE A PLAY

The first thing we should bear in mind is that if a thing is worth doing, it is worth doing well; and if we are to produce our play well, there is a great deal of work to be done.

CHOICE OF PLAY

We first choose our play, and this must be done with care. Our play should be a good one and it should be suitable for the players who are going to perform it. It should not be too difficult for them to understand, nor too difficult for them to act. It should also be suitable for the acting-space in which it is to be performed. For instance, if we have only a very small stage, it would be foolish to choose a play with fifty characters and ten elaborate changes of scene! You can imagine what would happen!

SHARING OUT THE WORK

Having chosen our play, we must next appoint the PRODUCER. Since he will be in complete command, it is important that he should be someone who has considerable knowledge of acting, is a good organizer and is able to make clear to the players exactly what he wants them to do. The Producer should have a large share in the next step, which is called 'casting' the play. This means choosing the actors who are to play the various parts. Often this task is left entirely to the Producer who, after all, knows exactly the type of person he needs to play each part. To help him to choose, he might hold what are called 'auditions', at which various people read a few lines from the play before it is finally decided who shall play any particular part.

At this point we should also choose the Stage Manager. The STAGE MANAGER is in charge of the stage. He supervises the putting-up and taking-down of the scenery (called 'setting' and 'striking' respectively), the placing of the furniture and properties, and he ensures that the electrician has carried out the wishes of the Producer with regard to lighting. He is responsible for seeing that the players are present and ready to make their entrances at the proper time and, in short, his work is to eliminate 'hitches' and ensure the smooth running of the play. All the members of the stage staff work directly under his orders whilst he himself, of course, takes his orders from the Producer. In large productions the Stage Manager sometimes has an Assistant Stage Manager to help him.

The stage staff consists of:

1. *The Property Master* whose job is to collect together and take charge of all the things used in the play (called 'properties' or 'props' for short) such as swords, trays, telephones, letters, teapots, newspapers, etc. There are two kinds of 'props':

(i) *Hand-props* which are small things carried by the actors in their hands, pockets or handbags. The Property Master must see that each actor is carrying the props he needs before he goes on the stage, and, as the actor leaves the stage, he should hand the props back to the Property

How to Produce a Play

Master. This is important to the smooth running of the play. Often the action of a play has broken down because one of the actors has forgotten to bring on something he needs.

(ii) *Stage-props* which are the properties already on the stage (or on the side ready to be taken on) before the curtain rises. The Property Master should check all the stage-props beforehand so that when, for instance, an actor goes to pick up a dagger from a table, he knows the dagger will be there.

The first thing the Property Master should do is to read the play carefully and make a Property List—that is, he should write down a list of all the properties, both hand and stage-props, needed in the play.

2. *The Stage Carpenter.* He sometimes builds the scenery and helps to make some of the properties. He also carries out any repairs to the set which may be necessary.

3. *The Electrician.* He is in charge of the lights and arranges them according to the wishes of the Producer. Not only does he fix up the lights, but also works them during the performance, dimming, brightening or changing them as and when necessary.

4. *The Effects Man.* He is responsible for what are called 'noises off'—that is, sounds made out of sight of the audience such as knocks on doors, bells ringing, noises of motor-cars or trains, birds singing and so on. Some of the sound effects may be made manually—that is, with the hands, as, for instance, imitating the sound of a horse galloping by knocking together two half-coconut shells—others may be produced by using gramophone records. These may be bought from Bishop Sound and Electrical Co., Ltd., 48 Monmouth Street,

How to Produce a Play

London, W.C.2. Their catalogue contains a large number of sound effects ranging from a horse walking to a full-scale air-raid!

5. *The Prompter*. The prompter sits at the side of the stage hidden from the audience. His job is to prompt the actors when they forget their lines. He should try to speak so that he is heard by the actor but not by the audience. If the play is going as it should, his services will not be required at all.

6. *The Call Boy*. His job is to summon the actors from the dressing-rooms so that they are on the side of the stage and ready to make their entrances in good time. He usually works under orders from the Stage Manager, but, sometimes, from the Prompter, who has before him the script on the margin of which should be pencilled, 'Call Lord Darcy' or, 'Call King' about a page or so before these characters are due to make their entrances.

7. *The Stage Hands*. These are the people who make themselves generally useful by setting or striking the scenery, moving the furniture and so on. They work directly under the Stage Manager.

The work of all the above people is important to the smooth running of the play. They should all wear rubber shoes or plimsolls and learn to move about noiselessly. Also, they should remember not to talk above a whisper during the performance of the play and never allow themselves to be seen by the audience.

If we are having any scenery, we shall require ARTISTS to design and paint it, and we shall also need a WARDROBE MISTRESS to look after the costumes. Should we decide to make our own costumes, more artists would be required to design them and SEMPSTRESSES to help to make them. All the designs for scenery and costumes should be submitted to the Producer for his approval before proceeding further with them.

If you are producing a simple play with relatively few characters and no complicated scene changes, most of the foregoing tasks can be 'telescoped'—that is, one person can perform the functions of two or three of these people. For instance, one person might act as Stage Manager, Electrician and Stage Carpenter. Another might combine the tasks of Effects Man, Property Master and Scenic Artist. All the Stage Staff could lend a hand with the setting and striking of the scenery. It matters little if there are only two or three of you— the various tasks can be shared out as is most convenient. Also, any of the actors who have only small parts can usually make themselves useful behind the scenes in various ways under the direction of the Producer.

REHEARSALS

Now we come to the play itself. The Producer should study the script very thoroughly. He should first picture the whole thing in his 'mind's eye' and try to determine how the Author would wish the play to be performed. He should have a clear picture of the kind of person each character is intended to be and know where the 'high-spots' or climaxes of the play occur and how to 'put them over' effectively. He should decide which passages of the play should be played quickly, which should be played slowly and where pauses should occur. He should plan the positions of the players, when they are to move, where they are to move, and how they are to move, and try to arrange these moves so that they form a series of inter-

How to Produce a Play

esting groupings, melting from one to another throughout the play. It is possible, of course, that the Producer will change and improve these moves as rehearsals proceed.

When the Producer knows exactly what he wants, it is time to begin rehearsals, which should proceed along the following lines:

1. *A 'Read-Through'*

The players sit round in a group and each reads his or her lines. The Producer reads the 'stage-directions'.

By this means the players get a general idea of the play, whilst the Producer has the opportunity of discussing with the actors the various characters they are to portray—what kind of people they are and how they would behave. A wise Producer does not tell an actor how to interpret his part—he leaves it to the actor to study and feel the part and interpret it in his own way. The Producer's job is not to teach the actor how to act, but to bring out and develop the actor's skill and guide it so that it fits artistically into the general plan.

How to Produce a Play

2. A 'Walk-Through'

In this rehearsal, the players, still reading from the scripts, begin to move about and learn their positions. It is necessary now to have the positions of the furniture marked either by real furniture or by boxes or by anything suitable which happens to be on hand. It may be necessary to have several 'walk-through' rehearsals.

3. Study

The players should now learn their lines thoroughly. When learning a part, it is useful to have a friend to read the 'cues' for us. The 'cues' are the few words at the end of the speeches which come just before *our* speeches. When we hear the cue, it should remind us of what to say next.

4. Full Rehearsals

We now should rehearse the whole play without scripts. The Producer may require us to go over certain difficult parts of the play more often until we get them right.

1

A Proscenium, or 'Picture-frame' stage

2

A Semi-Arena

3

An Arena

How to Produce a Play

5. *Dress Rehearsal*

This is a full rehearsal with costumes, make-up, scenery, properties and lighting—just as it is to be at the actual performance. It is often found that one or two snags have arisen and now is the time for the Producer to put them right.

THE PERFORMANCE

All the time that rehearsals have been proceeding, the artists, costume-makers, scenery-builders and stage-staff have been busy, and now we come to the climax of our project—the actual performance. If we have all done our best with zest and enthusiasm, we shall thoroughly enjoy ourselves, and let us hope the audience will enjoy themselves too!

STAGE POSITIONS

Your play may be produced on—

1. A proscenium, or 'picture-frame' stage—the usual kind,

or 2. A semi-arena,

or 3. An arena.

As most plays are produced on the proscenium stage, it is necessary to learn the accepted stage positions which are referred to in the stage-directions of most plays. The following diagram will explain them. In the script they are usually abbreviated, and these shortened forms are given in brackets on the diagram.

On arena and semi-arena stages, the positioning and movement of the players is usually left entirely to the Producer.

How to Produce a Play

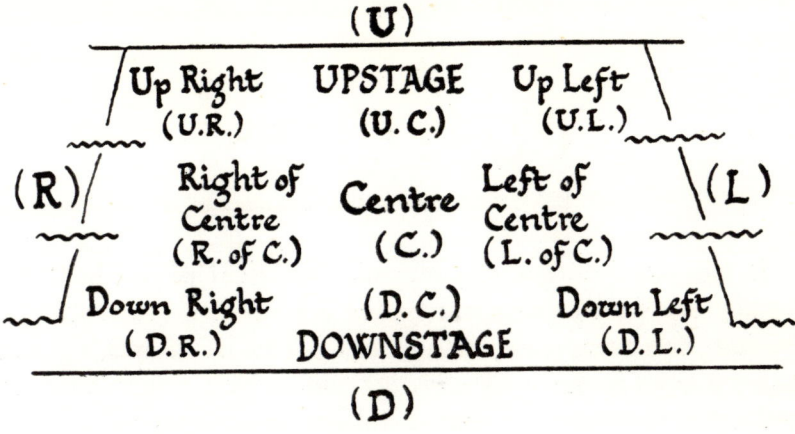

Audience

COSTUMES

If you are producing a serious, historical play where accuracy of detail is important, it is best to hire the costumes. Hiring, however, is expensive, and it can be interesting and enjoyable to make your own costumes. You might start by collecting together a 'dressing-up' box containing all kinds of old garments, coloured stockings, hats and scarves. These will do for your first efforts. Later you might make a few 'basic costumes' from hessian—loose, smock-like garments, some long, some short, to which brightly coloured pieces of material can quickly be sewn. The pictures show how one simple garment can be made to represent several costumes.

Cloaks, long and short, are always useful, and crowns and helmets can be made from cardboard, fastened with paper-fasteners and painted with gold or silver paint. Berets can form the basis of several kinds of headgear and a collection of plumes and feathers can be used to decorate them. It is always useful, too, to have an assortment of wands, swords, daggers and battle-axes handy. All these can be made from canes, broom-handles, bits of wood, cardboard and paint.

Quite realistic chain mail can be knitted in thick string on large needles and painted with silver paint.

When designing costumes let your designs be bold, simple and colourful. Small, finicky details are not effective and often cannot be seen at all from the audience.

Costumes

Not all plays, however, are set in the past. Many are set in the present and when these plays are in rehearsal, we sometimes hear it said, 'You won't have to trouble about costume. You can just wear your own clothes. Anything will do.' This is a mistake. 'Anything' will *not* do! Just as much care, attention and thought should be given to the dressing of a modern play as would be given to the most elaborate historical production.

Each costume should carry a definite message. It should tell the audience, at a glance, what kind of person you are —whether you are precise and business-like (bowler hat, striped trousers, rolled umbrella) or artistic (sandals, paint-bespattered trousers, gaily-coloured neckerchief, velvet jacket). Your costume should indicate whether you are fashion-conscious, or one of those people who wear clothes only for comfort and warmth; whether you are a person who likes to draw attention to himself, or one who is self-effacing; whether you are a person of good taste or a person of no taste; whether you are rich or poor, old or young, conventional or eccentric.

In many halls in which amateur productions take place, the part of the actor which is directly on the eye-level of the audience and therefore the first to be noticed, is his feet. And yet in dressing a play, too often it is the footwear that receives the least attention. Again, it is assumed that, since the play is modern, you may wear anything but, just as much as the rest of the costume, the footwear should be right for the character.

The colours of the dresses, in modern plays as much as in costume plays, should be chosen with care. They should blend with each other and with the colour-scheme of the set. This applies especially to the girls' costumes. A dress which

Costumes

clashes horribly with the background is distracting and irritating to the audience and so lowers the dramatic effect of the whole scene.

Far from lowering the dramatic effect, costume should play its part, together with the set, the lighting and the make-up, in building up the atmosphere and making an integral contribution to the clarity and unity of the overall dramatic picture.

5. Boys acting a mime about black magic and Zombies in the jungles of Martinique

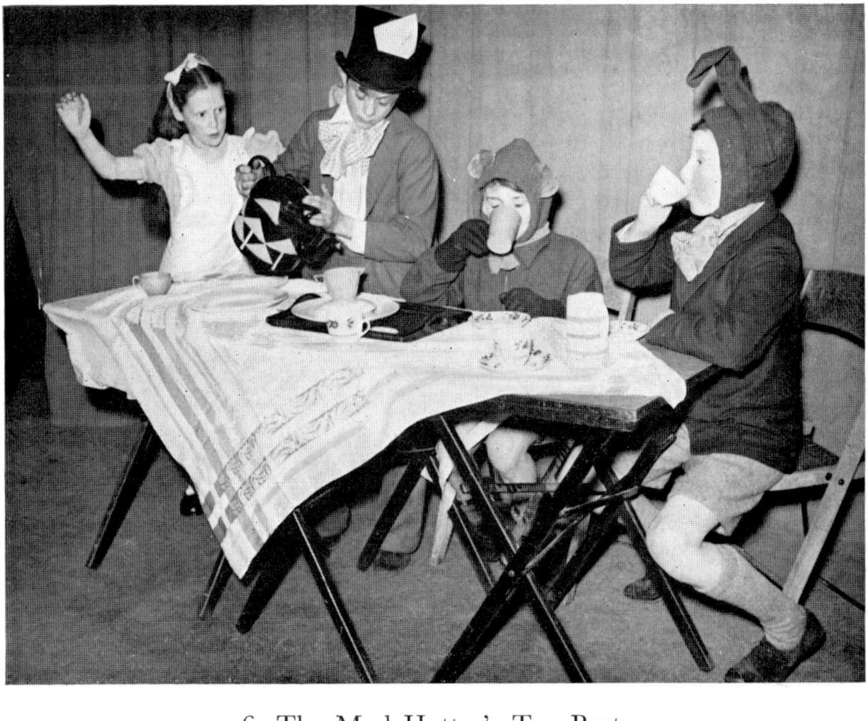

6. The Mad Hatter's Tea Party

7. 'The Producer should plan the positions of the players ... so that they form a series of interesting groupings.' Here is an example of such a grouping

8. A Youth Club's production of *Treasure Island* illustrating make-up, effective and dramatic lighting and the actors' 'feeling for the part'

MAKE-UP

Make-up is necessary on the stage because without it, and under strong stage lighting, a person looks pale, drab and uninteresting. Also it is often necessary to alter the appearance of an actor's face to make him look like the character he is portraying. Make-up can make you look older or younger; it can make your nose appear bigger or less; it can make your eyes appear bright or dull; it can make your cheeks appear full or hollow; it can make you look healthy or ill.

There are two kinds of make-up—

'Straight' make-up,

and 'Character' make-up.

'Straight' make-up is used when you wish to appear more or less as yourself.

'Character' make-up is used when you wish to alter your appearance.

The basis of make-up is grease-paint which is made in sticks. Every actor should have his own make-up box. If you wish to start one, you should buy the following things, which are all you need to begin with. Later, you can add to them if you wish.

Make-up

MAKE-UP BOX

Grease-paint:
>1 stick No. 5
>1 stick No. 9
>1 stick White
>1 stick Carmine
>1 black liner (a thin stick)
>1 lake liner
>1 blue liner

1 tin cold cream (cheap variety)
1 box powder (pale brownish—not white)
1 powder puff (or cotton wool)
1 bottle spirit gum, 1 small paint-brush
Crêpe hair—brown, fair, black, red, white or grey
Scissors
A few spent matches
A few clean rags or cotton wool

HOW TO DO A 'STRAIGHT' MAKE-UP

1. Wrap a towel round your neck to protect your costume.

2. Apply a *little* cold cream. Rub it in and wipe off the surplus with a towel or clean rag.

3. Take a grease-paint No. 5 and daub it all over your face and ears. (You need not cover the whole of the surface—cover most of it.) Now spread it over with the finger-tips, getting it perfectly smooth and even, not forgetting to go into the corners of the eyes and round the nostrils. Don't rub it in—spread it smoothly over.

4. Take a grease-paint No. 9 and repeat the operation,

Make-up

blending it into the No. 5 with your fingers. Avoid a hard edge under the chin. Shade it off, but don't take it too far down the neck or it will soil your costume.

5. The eyes. Take the black liner and draw a *very thin* line from the inner corner of the eye across the upper lid and along the very edge of it, touching the eye-lashes. Continue the line for about a quarter of an inch beyond the outer corner of the eye. Take the blue liner and place a few dabs on the lid itself. Smooth this over with a finger and shade it off beneath the eyebrow and at the sides. Now take a matchstick. Rub the clean end of it on the carmine grease-paint and place a small spot in the inner corner of each eye.

6. Boys—add a little more No. 9 to the cheeks and shade it off smoothly all round. Girls—add a few dabs of carmine to each cheek and shade it off smoothly—chiefly in an upward and outward direction towards the temples. *Don't put on too much red.*

7. Take the powder puff and dab plenty of powder all over your face. Keep dabbing and smoothing lightly until the surface is perfectly smooth and matt and the colour of the grease-paint shows through. When you have finished there should be no 'shine' showing from the grease-paint underneath.

8. It is not always necessary to touch the eyebrows at all. If you wish to darken them slightly, use the black liner and darken *the hairs* a little—not the skin underneath.

Make-up

9. Girls—paint your lips fairly thickly with carmine. Boys—just wipe the powder off your lips with a finger.

10. Do your hair.

To remove the make-up, apply plenty of cold cream, vaseline or liquid paraffin. Rub well all over the face and wipe with a clean rag or cotton wool. Don't try to wash it off with water.

CHARACTER MAKE-UP

It is impossible in a book of this size to attempt to describe all the various types of character make-up. Here, however, are a few tips:

Wrinkles. Follow the natural wrinkles of your face. Using a lake liner, draw the wrinkles *thinly*. Now take a matchstick. Rub it on the white grease-paint and draw white lines immediately below and touching the lake lines. Dab lightly with a finger to smooth. Wrinkles are usually drawn on the forehead, from the outer corners of the eyes (called 'crow's feet') and from the hollows at the outer edge of the nostril to below the corners of the mouth. Darkening the areas under the eyes with lake, that is, making 'bags' under the eyes, helps to make you look old, worn or ill.

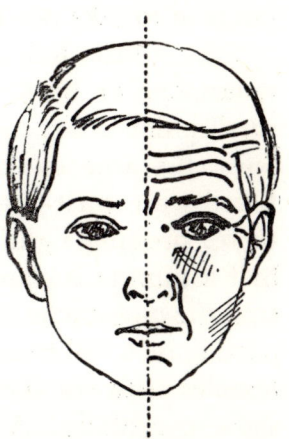

White Hair. You can make your own hair white by using white grease-paint and powder.

Wigs. When wearing a wig, be sure to disguise the join across the forehead by daubing it over thickly with No. 5

Make-up

and No. 9 grease-paint and smoothing it up on to the wig itself. Stick the edge of the wig to the temples with spirit gum if it is inclined to gape.

Chins. Chins can be made to look rough and unshaven by blending blue and black and smoothing over and up the cheeks to the hair.

Noses and cheeks. A nose can be made to appear to stand out by using No. 5 and, possibly, a little white thickly down the centre of the ridge and darkening with No. 9 the sides. Smooth the edges. Cheek bones, too, can be made to appear prominent in a similar way.

Moustaches and beards. These are made of crêpe hair which is sold in plaits. First unplait the hair and iron it with a fairly hot iron to take out the 'crimp'. It is now ready for use.

Take a little hair and roughly fashion it into the shape of moustache or beard required. Lay it down. Now, using a small paint-brush such as you use with water-colour paints, paint the area of skin to be covered by the moustache or beard with spirit gum. Place the hair in position and hold it there, pressing tightly with a damp rag or towel. In about half a minute it should be stuck. Now take the scissors and trim the moustache or beard into the shape desired. If you are putting on a full beard, be careful not to leave a gap near the temples between the beard and your own hair or this will show dreadfully! A surprisingly small amount of hair is needed to make a moustache.

Don't be discouraged if your first attempts at make-up are not very successful. Plenty of practice is needed to make a competent make-up artist.

LIGHTING

In Georgian times, before the days of electricity, stage-lighting presented a serious problem. Light was provided by candles and in order to provide sufficient light for the actors to be seen an enormous number of candles was needed. These were concealed in every possible place—along the front, over the top and down the sides of the stage.

Nowadays, thanks to electricity and modern equipment, stage-lighting is very much more efficient and provides much more beautiful and varied effects. In the early part of this century the principal pieces of lighting equipment were battens (rows of lights suspended above the stage) and floats or footlights (a row of lights along the front edge of the stage). These are now out of favour. Footlights, a relic of the candle-days, are quite unnecessary. They give the set a flat and uninteresting appearance and, because they shine upwards from the floor, they throw unnatural shadows on to the actors' faces, making them look unreal and grotesque. Also, they cast huge unwanted shadows on to the backcloth or cyclorama. So, if your stage has footlights, remove them, place them upstage and use them to shine upwards on to your backcloth. They then become what is known as a groundrow and must, of course, be hidden from the audience by a rostrum or a piece of low, cut-out scenery.

Lighting

Your main source of light should be provided by spotlights. These should be placed in rows above the stage, taking the place of the first two rows of the old battens, and at each side of the auditorium, about eight or ten feet from the proscenium. These 'front-of-house' lights will leave a small unlit triangle downstage centre as shown in the diagram, and this dark triangle should be lit by another spotlight hung above and in front of the stage.

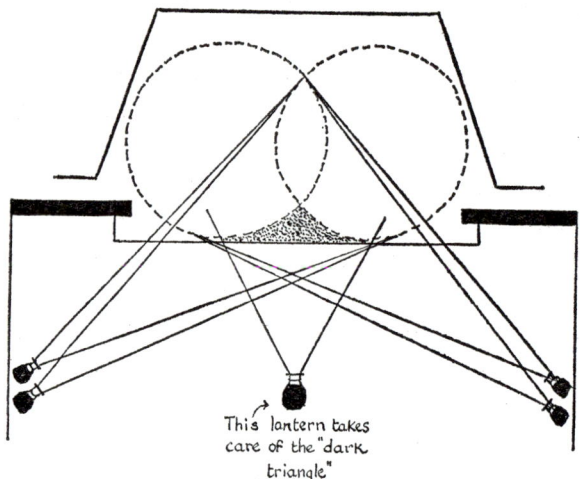

This lantern takes care of the "dark triangle"

The number of lanterns used will depend on the size of the stage, but bear in mind that two 250-watt lanterns are better than one 500-watt. The bigger the area to be lit, the more lanterns are required.

The 'front-of-house' or F.O.H. spots should be of the mirror-profile-type. These project, through a lens, a hard-edged profile of any shape you wish—circular, square, diamond—

A—F.O.H. spots (mirror profile). B—No. 1 barrel (Fresnel spots). C—No. 2 barrel (Fresnel spots). D—Old battens left in place to illuminate backcloth or cyclorama from above. E—Old floats used to illuminate backcloth or cyclorama from below.

Lighting

the shape being governed by a cut-out aperture inserted in the gate behind the lens. Using this type of lamp, you are able to direct all the beam on to the acting-area and avoid having stray light striking the proscenium and reflecting into the auditorium, which is distracting. If you do not yet possess mirror-profile spots and have to use ordinary focus-lanterns, then you will have to fix 'barn-doors' in front of the lanterns, above, below and on each side of the lenses to 'kill' the stray light on the proscenium.

The spots used on the stage itself should be of the soft-edged Fresnel type. This gives a soft-edged, circular beam with a gradual transition of intensity from the centre to outside edges. The beam is adjustable and can be used to illuminate a small spot or a large area.

All the lanterns can be trained to shine in the direction you desire, and you obtain the effect you want by experimenting, not only with direction and intensity, but also with colour. Colour-filters can be inserted in all lanterns. Avoid strong colours except for special effects. Use straws, pinks and ambers for a warm effect; blues, greens and greys for a cold effect.

Another type of lantern is the floodlight which, as its name suggests, sheds a flood of light over a wide area. This type is not used so often nowadays, as Fresnel spots can do the job just as efficiently and are much less clumsy.

A few spot-lamps on stands placed on the stage are useful for throwing an intensity of light on one spot to simulate the pool of light from a candle, oil-lamp or standard lamp which forms part of the set. They can also be used to simulate sunshine or moonlight shining through a window.

All lamps should be connected to a control-board which should have dimmer-banks. Eight dimmer-banks, each taking

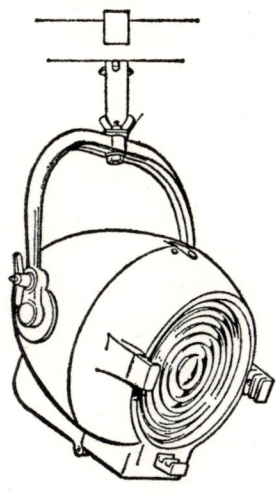
Soft edge Fresnel spot

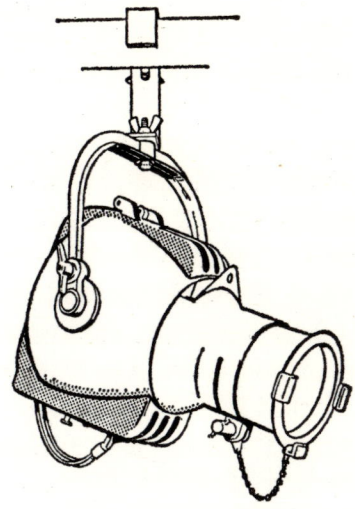
Mirror profile spot

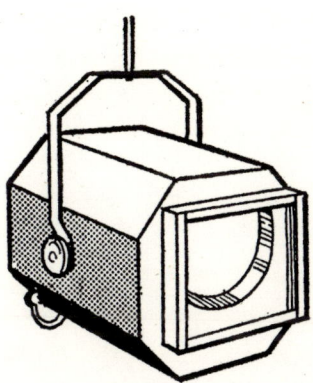
Focus lantern

Lighting

1 kilowatt, should be sufficient for the ordinary school or hall stage. The cable connecting the control-board to the mains should be heavy enough to take the maximum load of the board, and the connection should be done by a competent electrician with the consent of the local electricity authority.

The lighting should help to emphasize the mood and atmosphere of the play. Equipment can be hired very reasonably from Strand Electric, 29 King Street, London W.C.2, or W. J. Furse & Co. Ltd., 20 Traffic Street, Nottingham, but it is better to buy your equipment, a bit at a time if necessary, gradually adding to your stock until you have an efficient and adaptable lighting system. With the basic arrangement described above, it is possible to achieve an almost limitless variety of effects. By experimenting with colour, with varied intensities of light from different sources (using the dimmers) and with the use of various combinations of the lanterns, you are able to discover the full potential of the arrangement and find just the right effect for any particular scene.

Finally, a word of warning—never allow naked flames (candles, torches or oil-lamps) on the stage. The risk of fire from them, especially in the tense excitement of the performance, is very great.

Lighting

'Flat' lighting   Imaginative lighting

Lighting should help to emphasize the mood and atmosphere

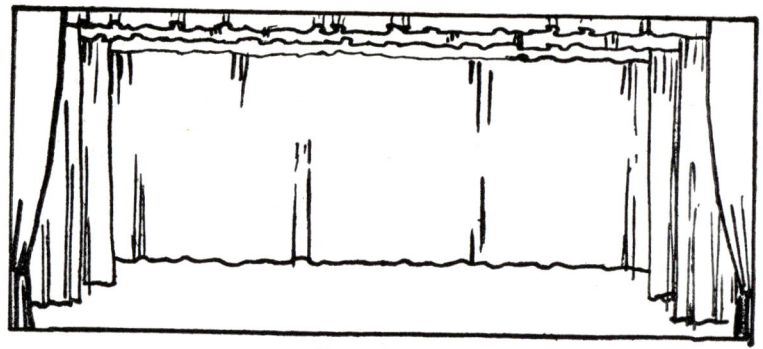

Curtain Set

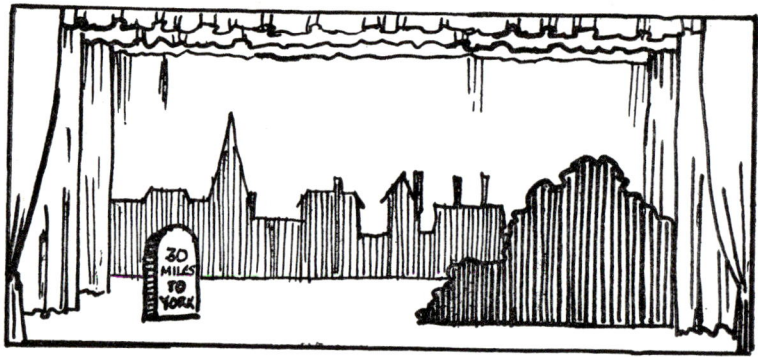

Use of 'cut-outs' with curtain set

Use of rostra, steps and screens with curtain set giving varying acting-levels

MAKING YOUR OWN PLAY

Choosing a play to produce can be an exasperating business! You read play after play without finding just the one you want. You could, of course, persevere and go on reading still more plays, but there is an alternative. Why not write your own play? It can be interesting work, and, what is more, you can so fashion your play that it is suitable for the stage, the actors and the props and apparatus you happen to have available.

For your first attempts at performing an original play you need not rely on written dialogue at all. If you know the story, you can make up the words as you go along, just as you used to do when you played Pirates or Cowboys and Indians. Later, you can write the play down on paper, learn the lines and produce it properly, thus improving your first efforts.

Performing a play is merely a fascinating and exciting way of telling a story, so your play must have a story, or plot. Remember, too, that your play must work up to a high point of excitement or dramatic interest. This 'high spot' is called the CLIMAX. The climax may occur near the end, at the very end,

Making Your Own Play

or in the middle. Seldom does it occur near the beginning because of the difficulty of sustaining the interest for a long time after the moment of greatest excitement has passed. Sometimes, in longer plays, we find several minor climaxes before we reach the major and final climax.

You must also bear in mind that to make a play dramatic and alive it must express CONFLICT in some way. The conflict may take the form of a physical fight, it may be a quarrel or argument, it may be the conflict of loyalties or the conflict of ideas.

Try to make the dialogue sound natural by making each character use the kind of language he would normally use were he real and alive. It is a good idea to read your dialogue over to yourself aloud, or, alternatively, get a friend to read it aloud to you. You then have a much clearer idea of how it will sound when the play is performed, and can make any alterations and improvements which seem to be necessary. The awkward or clumsy bits, you will find, are much more easily detected by the ear than by the eye.

Don't allow your characters to sit or stand about talking in one position for too long. Make them move about and get some action into the play. Otherwise, unless you are extremely clever at writing witty and entertaining dialogue, there is a danger that your play may become tedious.

Here are two outline plots which you can translate into plays for yourself. This will give you practice in adapting a narrative to play-form:

Making Your Own Play

GRANNIE CHANGES HER MIND

A Comedy in One Act

Characters

Grannie Stratton, a crotchety old lady.
Mr. Stratton, her son.
Mrs. Stratton, her daughter-in-law.
Peter Stratton, her grandson, aged sixteen.
Penny Stratton, her grand-daughter, aged thirteen.
Mrs. Walker, a gossip-loving neighbour.

SCENE: The living-room of Mr. and Mrs. Stratton's house.

When the curtain rises we see Grannie sitting in her armchair by the fire. She is knitting a scarf for Penny. Mrs. Stratton is darning socks by the table and Mr. Stratton, in another easy chair, is reading the evening paper.

Grannie has dropped a stitch, and, complaining about her failing eyesight, asks Mrs. Stratton to pick it up for her. Mrs. Stratton does so. Grannie goes on grumbling for some time, recalling the days when she was young and had such good eyesight that she could sew a finer hem than anyone she knew. This reminds her of the short-comings of the younger generation. She compares the needlework she used to do with the handiwork of young Penny, and goes on to complain of the careless, slipshod, scatter-brained goings-on of children nowadays. Mrs. Stratton occasionally tries to put in a good word for the children, but Mr. Stratton remains apparently deeply immersed in his newspaper.

Making Your Own Play

Penny comes in. We learn that she has been out to see a friend. Mr. Stratton asks her if she remembered to post a letter he had given her. She says yes, she remembered. Her father asks her if she also remembered to buy a stamp from the Post Office and stick it on the letter before posting it. Alas! Penny has forgotten about the stamp! Mr. Stratton is annoyed. Grannie bursts in with 'What did I tell you?' She continues to enlarge on her pet theme until she is interrupted by the sound of the front-door bell.

It is Mrs. Walker, a neighbour, who has dropped in for a chat. After a little introductory conversation about the weather, Mrs. Walker gets down to the real purpose of her visit, which is to carry home a little malicious gossip about Peter. Putting on an air of 'I don't like to talk about people, but I think you ought to know', she describes how Mrs. Robinson has seen Peter climbing over the railway fence by the station, how Mrs. Jones saw him annoying the Mayor as he was leaving the Town Hall after a Council Meeting, and how she herself, with her own eyes, saw him chasing Mr. Lorrimer's hens and scaring the poor things to death!

All this gives Grannie another opportunity of deploring the lack of manners and morals in modern boys. She insists that young people in her day possessed much stronger characters—above all, they showed initiative, a quality sadly lacking today! *They* never got up to all this mischief! *They* could find better things to do, etc., etc., etc.

Mrs. Stratton again tries to take a reasonable view and several times appeals to her husband, but he refuses to be drawn and keeps his own counsel.

At this point Peter arrives. Mr. Stratton at once rouses

Making Your Own Play

himself and takes charge of the situation. Now that Peter is here to answer for himself, says he, let him be confronted with these tales instead of having them whispered behind his back. Mrs. Walker's accusations are repeated to Peter who admits the truth of them all! At this confession, Mrs. Walker is smugly self-righteous, Grannie is triumphant and Mr. and Mrs. Stratton are puzzled and worried.

Then Peter goes on to say that there is a perfectly simple explanation—he was merely taking part in an Initiative Test organized by his Scout Troop. One of his tasks was to obtain the Mayor's signature on a punched platform ticket. That was why he had to leave the station in a rather unconventional manner and why he was seen badgering the Mayor. Another of his tasks was to bring back the tail-feather of a Rhode Island cockerel which he had obtained from Mr. Lorrimer's flock with the permission of their owner!

At this moment the telephone-bell rings. Mr. Stratton answers it. The Scoutmaster has telephoned to give the news that Peter has won the first prize for obtaining the highest number of marks in the Initiative Test and that he is to receive an inscribed cup!

Mrs. Walker is crestfallen! She is even more embarrassed when Grannie now changes sides completely, praising Peter for his initiative and adventurousness, and proudly boasting that he is a real Stratton—a chip of the old block! She declares that she always knew he had it in him and she is surprised and disgusted that Mrs. Walker should be so lacking in appreciation of the qualities of the Stratton family as to come sneaking along with such wicked and malicious gossip! Mrs. Walker bridles, makes a half-hearted attempt to justify her actions, but retires, defeated and abashed!

Making Your Own Play

A DEBT REPAID

A Play in One Act

Characters

Señor Manuella, a rich merchant.
Roderigo, Chief of a band of brigands.
Marco, his lieutenant.
José, a young brigand.
Other members of the brigand band (male and female).

Scene: A brigand's lair in the mountains near Seville.

Time: Early in the nineteenth century.

The brigand's lair is a rocky grotto high up in the mountains. On either side the rocks tower high. In the background can be seen an expanse of sky, giving the impression of a steep drop over the edge of the mountain ledge. A camp fire smoulders in the centre. The brigands are sitting or lying here and there. In one corner a card game is in progress. Others are playing dice. One man guards the entrance to the grotto. He stands in the background, silhouetted against the sky, leaning on his rifle and gazing down into the valley.

The guard gives the alarm—someone is approaching. The brigands immediately become alert. One or two join the guard and peer down the mountain slope. There appear to be three people coming. Soon, two of them are recognized as Roderigo, the brigand chief, and his lieutenant, Marco. In a

Making Your Own Play

few moments these two enter, bringing with them the third person—an elderly man, blindfolded and with his wrists tied together. Roderigo is jubilant. He has captured a fine prize, he exclaims, and introduces to his companions his prisoner—a rich merchant from Seville. He is to be held for ransom and the price of his release will be high! The brigands congratulate Roderigo and Marco on their excellent work.

Soon the brigands go off together on a raiding expedition. José, the youngest member of the band, is left to guard the prisoner. The two get into conversation. The merchant tries to persuade José to allow him to escape, but the boy remains staunch and loyal to the band. The merchant then gradually leads the conversation round to José's early life. José, dropping into a reminiscent mood, tells how, at a very early age, he was abandoned by his parents who were wandering gypsies—how he lived by begging and stealing and how, in these circumstances, he came to feel that the whole world was against him and, particularly, those in authority. There was, however, one bright spot which shone like a star in the dark sky of José's life. This was the period when, for a few months, he was taken into the home of a kind gentleman and his wife. They had given him care and affection and this was the only pure, good and happy memory he possessed. He had, for a short time, experienced another world—a world of comfort, security and refinement. Whether it was weakness of character, or whether his gypsy blood prevented his settling down, he did not know, but he stole money from his kind benefactor and ran away—an action he ever afterwards bitterly regretted.

The merchant then asks José to remove the bandage from his eyes. José, curiously moved by some quality in the merchant's voice, obeys. He looks into the merchant's eyes and recognizes Señor Manuella, his one-time benefactor and protector! Overcome with emotion and torn between loyalty to his companions and gratitude to his former friend, José eventually realizes that he must assist Señor Manuella to escape. A plan is devised. José will lead the Señor down the mountain by the secret path, then hurry back and pretend the prisoner freed himself and put a drug in José's wine which sent him to sleep. José frees the Señor and they are just about to start when Roderigo emerges suddenly from behind a rock. His horse having shed a shoe, he had returned on foot. Hearing the conversation, he had listened and had overheard the whole plan. Treachery, he exclaims, merits but one punishment, and that is death!

Señor Manuella pleads for José's life, but Roderigo is adamant. He draws a pistol and points it at José. As he fires, Señor Manuella throws himself in front of the terrified boy and receives the bullet in his shoulder. José, thinking his friend dead, seizes a knife from his belt. He leaps at the bandit chief and stabs him to the heart! Then, mourning over his friend, he discovers that the Señor is not dead, but only wounded. Carefully he lifts him on to his shoulder and carries him out of the grotto and down the mountain side.

Next, here is the *beginning* of a plot which you can complete yourself. You may introduce other characters if you wish.

The scene is a cell-like room in the Tower of London. The period is Elizabethan. At the table sits Sir Robert Wilkin. By the light of a candle he is writing in his journal. He speaks the words as he writes, telling how he has been imprisoned by the Queen and condemned to death for plotting to put Mary of

Making Your Own Play

Scotland on the English throne. He passionately declares his innocence, saying he is a man of peace and that his only wish was to remove the enmity between Elizabeth and Mary, and, consequently, between England and Scotland. He wonders if his appeal for clemency has been successful.

The door opens and a Bishop enters, accompanied by Sir William Adams and Sir Henry Swale, high officers of the Queen's Court. The Bishop tells Sir Robert that his appeal has failed and that he is to die at dawn the next day. It appears that the appeal has just been heard in the precincts of the Tower and that the Queen is still in the building. On hearing this, Sir Robert begs that he might be allowed to send a note to Her Majesty. As a last request, this is granted. He writes the note which is taken by Sir Henry. A few minutes later, Queen Elizabeth herself bursts into the room. She is accompanied by her ladies and holds the note in her hand. Her face is white and strained. 'I think, Sir Robert, you had better tell me more of this matter,' she says, and sends everyone except the prisoner out of the room.

Now finish the story and make it into a play.

Here is the description of a scene and a list of characters:

Scene

A glade in a forest. Up L. is the ivy-clad wall of a ruined church. Part of the tracery of a Gothic window remains and through this the moon is shining on to a grassy bank, R.C. Here, covered in old newspapers, lies Harry, asleep. Stars are visible in the night sky between the tree-trunks. It is an hour before dawn on a May morning.

Making Your Own Play

Characters

Harry, the tramp.
Tom Burnett, a game-keeper.
Betty, his daughter.
An old beggar-woman.
A Stranger, who turns out to be the Spirit of Father Ignatius, who, four hundred years ago, was the Abbot of the Monastery of which the ruined wall is the only remaining relic.

Now, imagine what might happen to these people in this setting, and make it into a play.

Now make up a play using the following characters. Use your imagination to supply the scene and the plot.

Characters

Mr. Basil Lock, the late Miss Charity Perkins's solicitor.
George,
Edward,
Eleanor, } her nephews and nieces.
Gloria,
Dr. Hartford, her physician and old friend.
Miss Pimm, her late companion.
Mary, her old servant.
Oswald Smee, a distant relative recently returned from Canada.

Making Your Own Play

Next, supply the characters, scenes and plots of plays with the following titles:

The Mystery of the Grandfather Clock.
The Biter Bit!
'Binko's Marvellous Rejuvenator!'
A Rolling Stone Comes to Rest.
Midsummer Madness.
The Christmas Ghost of Engleby Grange.

Lastly, you might find it interesting to translate incidents from history or literature into plays. Alternatively, you might write a wholly original play, you being the sole creative artist, supplying title, scene, characters, and plot entirely from your own wits and imagination.

IMPROVISED DRAMA

Throughout the book so far, we have considered acting in plays which are to be performed before an audience. We have studied the various things we should do to ensure that our efforts look and sound well to the spectators. We have learned that to 'put over' a play successfully, we must accept certain disciplines and acquire certain techniques.

There is, however, another kind of drama which is becoming increasingly popular and has nothing whatever to do with audiences. This is improvised drama in which the actors make up the words (and, sometimes, the plot) as they go along. There is no need to learn parts off by heart—there is no script. There is no need to think of 'projection' for there is no audience to project to. Improvised drama can be done by you alone, in twos, in small groups or in large groups. All you need in the way of equipment is a space—a hall floor, a lawn, a field, a wood—and a few rostra, steps or old boxes and packing-cases to represent all kinds of things from the deck of a ship to a mountain peak! You may 'dress up' or not, as you wish, but if you do wear costume, it is not because it 'looks well from the audience', but because the wearing of it helps you to feel you really are the character you are acting.

In the Introduction, you may remember, reference was made to the imaginative games you used to play when you

Improvised Drama

were younger—the games when you were cowboys or nurses or housewives. (For all I know, you may still enjoy such games!) These games, as the Introduction says, formed a normal part of 'growing-up'. You were trying out situations and actions which might occur at a later stage of your life. In exactly the same way, young animals play acting-games which help to educate them for their future lives as mature creatures. Kittens chase and pounce on any quickly-moving object as they will chase and pounce on a mouse when they are older. Puppies worry and shake an old slipper as they will worry and shake a rat later in life.

Although your imaginative games undoubtedly had value, as a form of expression they did not get you very far. They just went on and on, aimlessly and formlessly, until you were tired and felt like playing at something else. Improvised drama takes your natural instinct for acting and gives it form and purpose—form, because the stories you act will have a beginning, a middle and an end; purpose because the activity will be doing you good in many ways. It is true self-expression. You are expressing *your* thoughts and *your* feelings rather than those of a playwright. And, by expressing your ideas, you learn to evaluate them. Vague impressions become clear and sharp, confusing impressions sort themselves out and frightening impressions are squarely faced and lose their terrors. Also, by 'being' other people, you begin to see things as others see them, to feel as others feel, to react as others react and so become more understanding, more tolerant, more compassionate.

Because it has been found to be so valuable, improvisation is often used in drama schools where students are being trained for the stage, and even film-makers have experi-

Improvised Drama

mented with improvised dialogue because it adds realism to the scene.

All acting stems from feeling and this applies especially to improvisation. The most important thing is to become, for the time being, the character you are portraying. You speak as he does, you move as he does, you feel and react as he does because you *are he*! This is called 'absorption' and means becoming totally engrossed, mentally, emotionally and physically, in the character. Once this has been achieved, problems of shyness and self-consciousness vanish.

The most difficult thing is to make a start, and to help you to do this, you need something to capture your interest and rouse your imagination. There are many 'starters' or stimuli, as we may call them. The easiest is, perhaps, a story. You hear or read the story, you discuss it, you decide who is to play each character and what you will need (if anything) in the way of costume and props, then you act it, making up the words as you go along. You may take your story from literature (e.g. *The Pied Piper*), from the Bible (e.g. Joseph and his coat of many colours) or from history (e.g. the story of the Tolpuddle martyrs or a story about the Luddites, who destroyed new machinery in the mills because they thought it would throw them out of work). It is often interesting to delve into the history of your own town or village. Here you may well find a dramatic incident which you could enjoy acting. You might even act it on the actual site where it occurred.

Music is another form of stimulus. A piece of dramatic 'mood' music may conjure up images in your imagination from which a story might emerge. First, you listen carefully to the music with your eyes closed. Then you discuss it, each telling what mental pictures or actions it suggested. Some of

Improvised Drama

the music by Borodin, for example, might suggest a battle; Malcolm Arnold's overture *Tam O'Shanter* might suggest witches or hobgoblins; some of Tchaikovsky's music from *Swan Lake* might conjure up the vision of a princess gliding in a barge over moonlit water towards a dark tower.... From these impressions actable stories could emerge. All that remains is to cast the characters, arrange the acting-area, discuss the outline—the beginning, the middle and the end—and get on with it! If you play the music again whilst you are acting, you will find it will help your absorption.

Again, there are many pictures which could easily stimulate your imaginations and suggest a story to act. An illustration in a book or a picture hanging on a wall might very well set you thinking thoughts and feeling emotions which could be turned into an improvised play. Alternatively, simple domestic happenings and situations such as occur in your own lives—a wedding, a holiday, a visit to the zoo, a family quarrel—could all form the basis of improvised drama.

You might take the beginning of a story—man comes home late at night, looking forward to seeing wife and children, eating a good supper, putting on slippers and sitting in front of a roaring fire—but finds house in darkness, front door standing wide open. He goes into the hall—calls—no reply ... —begin to act it and see what happens as the story continues. (In this example, the wife and children could decide why the house is dark and silent but keep 'Father' in the dark about it, just to see how he reacts to the situation.)

In this kind of exercise you are, of course, not only making up the words as you go along, but also the plot. Or, perhaps, you may find that the plot takes over and makes *itself* up as the play proceeds! Whatever happens, you may be sure that

Improvised Drama

you will derive a great deal of pleasure from your activities and, once having got into the way of enjoying improvised drama, you will find that you want to repeat the experience again and again.